BRIAN JOHNSTON

# Abraham: Friend of God

# Contents

# 1

# LEAVING HOME

Away beyond the great River Euphrates in Mesopotamia about 2,000 years before Christ there once lived a man called Terah. Terah was a family man with three sons, one called Abram – or Abraham as he came to be known. They lived about ten generations after Noah. This family were city-dwellers. They lived in the city of Ur - close to the shoreline of the Persian Gulf, at one end of what's been described as the Fertile Crescent. At the other end was the Red Sea. The river valleys of the Tigris-Euphrates and Jordan rivers provided a great arc of richly irrigated land across this region. It seems cities of baked brick came to rise up along the length of these green river banks like shining objects glittering in a giant necklace.

Various sources all point in the direction of this being an area of ancient civilisation - with its cities crowned with stepped pyramids (called ziggurats) dedicated to patron deities. It's probable that the old capital of Sumer was Ur with its Temple of the Moon, so its people were moon-worshippers. From what we read in the book of Joshua (24:14) it might appear that Terah's family there were no exception. That is, until one day, quite out the blue it seems, they had an encounter with the true and living God. Life was never the same after that. Here from Genesis chapter 11 is the Bible record of these facts:

*"This is the genealogy of Terah: Terah begot Abram, Nahor, and Haran. Haran begot Lot. And Haran died before his father Terah in his native land, in Ur of the Chaldeans. Then Abram and Nahor took wives: the name of Abram's wife was Sarai ... But Sarai was barren; she had no child. And Terah took his son Abram and his grandson Lot, the son of Haran, and his daughter-in-law Sarai, his son Abram's wife, and they went out with them from Ur of the Chaldeans to go to the land of Canaan; and they came to Haran and dwelt there. So the days of Terah were two hundred and five years, and Terah died in Haran.*

*Now the LORD had said to Abram: 'Get out of your country, from your family and from your father's house, to a land that I will show you. I will make you a great nation; I will bless you and make your name great; and you shall be a blessing. I will bless those who bless you, and I will curse him who curses you; and in you all the families of the earth shall be blessed'"* (Genesis 11:27–12:3).

The security, sophistication and splendour of Ur, where life was good and comfortable, paled into insignificance compared to the revelation of 'the God of glory' that day. The New Testament reveals that this must actually have been the second time God had spoken to Abram - or Abraham. For Stephen (the first Christian martyr named in the Bible) said, just before he was stoned by the Jews, that:

> *"... the God of glory appeared to our father Abraham when he was in Mesopotamia, before he dwelt in Haran, and said to him, 'Get out of your country and from your relatives, and come to a land that I will show you.' Then he came out of the land of the Chaldeans and dwelt in Haran. And from there, when his father was dead, He moved him to this land in which you now dwell'"* (Acts 7:2-4).

So an ancient city-dweller had found God, or really, the sovereign God had found him. Abraham's initial reaction could have been 'why me?' Just before this time we read about the tower of Babel, when the nations of the earth had tried to undertake the monumental task of constructing a skyscraper by which they hoped to make a name for themselves, all the while excluding God from their thinking. The nations of the world had shut out the God of heaven; so, in turn, he shut them out, and began afresh with the selection of just one man - and that man was Abraham. Abraham's response to being selected for this kind of special revelation was quite radical. I suppose his attitude could have been one of 'Well, this is where I met God, so this must be where I should stay'. But God's revelation was an uncompromising command - to separate from his native land and relations (Acts 7:3).

It was to be the first of four far-reaching crises in his life; whereby, in turn, God would ask him to give up his country and relatives (Nahor stayed in Haran it would seem - Genesis 27); then to give up any thought of his nephew Lot becoming his adopted heir (Genesis 13); next to give up his son Ishmael, and abandon his own human strategies (Genesis 17); and fourthly, in a very real sense to even be willing to give up his special son Isaac - that which was precious beyond words to him (Genesis 22).

No wonder Abraham finds a prominent place in the eleventh chapter of the letter to the Hebrews - that chapter which some have called 'the gallery of the heroes of faith'. Great biblical men and women of faith are mentioned there along with a brief description of their exploits. But many verses are given over to Abraham. His response to these four crises of faith came to define his life with God - and God in his Word holds up Abraham's life as the classic example of a life of faith - the kind of faith that brings us into a relationship with God, and by which we can serve him acceptably. So Abraham was a separatist, for the revelation he'd received from God demanded he give up his country and relatives. He separated from the state-of-the-art civilisation in Mesopotamia with all it had to offer.

He became the founder of 'the Hebrews'. He's called 'Abram, the Hebrew' in Genesis chapter 14. A Hebrew means 'a crossed over one'. It's certainly a fitting description for someone who, in faith, crossed over 600 miles of Arabian Desert! Which is what happened, as we read on:

> *"So Abram departed as the LORD had spoken to him, and Lot went with him. And Abram was seventy-five years old when he departed from Haran. Then Abram took Sarai his wife and Lot his brother's son, and all their possessions that they had gathered, and the people whom they had*

*acquired in Haran, and they departed to go to the land of Canaan. So they came to the land of Canaan. Abram passed through the land to the place of Shechem, as far as the terebinth tree of Moreh. And the Canaanites were then in the land. Then the LORD appeared to Abram and said, 'To your descendants I will give this land.' And there he built an altar to the LORD, who had appeared to him. And he moved from there to the mountain east of Bethel, and he pitched his tent with Bethel on the west and Ai on the east; there he built an altar to the LORD and called on the name of the LORD. So Abram journeyed, going on still toward the South"* (Genesis 14:4-9).

We say again that if any word characterizes Abraham's relationship with God then that word is 'faith.' We read that Abraham *"believed in the LORD"* and that God *"accounted it to him for righteousness"* (Genesis 15:6). That's the type of response to knowing God that models for all time what God looks for in those who are to have a relationship with Him. Abraham left everything to follow the direction of the God of glory, while believing the promise that God would make him a great nation (Genesis 12:2). We're back to God's sovereignty again. In Genesis 11 the nations of the earth had shut out God, so in Genesis 12 God shuts out the nations, beginning again with one man - a man who turned from idols to become the friend of God. The God who was sidelined at Babel, turned to Abraham saying in effect: 'Come out from among them and be separate.'

Abraham's nephew, Lot, hadn't caught the separated vision, he drifted back to city-life and became ensnared by a Babylonian king (Genesis 13,14,18 &19). But the call of God had brought Abraham 'an inheritance' (Hebrews 11:8) - and that place was destined to become Israel's promised land in Canaan. Abraham the settled city-dweller became the nomadic tent-dweller, building altars to God wherever he went in the land of God's choice (Genesis 12:7). He became the classic pilgrim characterized by tent and altar on an awesome journey of faith. He didn't need to know his destination (Hebrews 11:8); it was enough that he knew God. The vision of the heavenly city - which was his ultimate destination - had eclipsed the glamour of city-life in Ur for good (Hebrews 11:10).

From his experience, recorded for our learning, we can discover classic features of a man or woman of God. For we, too, are pilgrims on an awesome journey of faith. After all, doesn't the apostle Peter (1 Peter 2:11) describe Christian believers as *"aliens and strangers"*? Like Abraham, we've known the call of God which has made us heirs of the same promise God made with Abraham (Hebrews 6:13-20) - like Isaac, we are 'children of promise' (Galatians 4:28), Paul says. *"And we, too, look for a heavenly city"*
; while down here in this life we're commanded to *"go out ... outside the camp"* (Hebrews 13:13) - the camp representing the place where human thoughts are exalted against God's thoughts. In all these ways - and more - we can relate to this larger-than-life Bible character.

# 2

# LEARNING FROM MISTAKES

God appeared to Abram when he was in Mesopotamia. That was just the first of other divine revelations which this early city-dweller-turned-nomad was to receive. The life of Abram as recorded in the Bible can, it seems, be divided into four stages. Each of them started with some sort of special revelation from God. First, there's his call and removal to Haran, as recounted in Genesis chapter 12. Then there's the time when he received from God the promise of a son and heir; that's in Genesis 15 and God makes a covenant with him there.

Some time later (Genesis 17), Abraham again has an encounter with God - one in which God changes his name from Abram to Abraham, renews his covenant with him, and gives him the token of circumcision. Then, the fourth period of Abram's life begins from the time he receives the most famous revelation of all. This is the time when God tests whether or not Abraham would be prepared to give up his long-awaited son, Isaac. These four outstanding revelations mark out the life of this man.

Of course, our main interest is what we can learn for ourselves from all this. We want to know how Abraham's experience of God can shape, or help us to understand better, our own experience of God. In trying to relate to a giant of faith like Abraham, it's good for us to notice that the Bible doesn't flatter its heroes. We get the full picture: warts and all. There were episodes in Abraham's life of which, I'm quite sure, he'd be ashamed - and they get an airing too. Man of faith though he undoubtedly was, Abraham was not without his lapses - just like any one of us. Take, for example, the time when:

*"... there was a famine in the land, and Abram went down to Egypt to dwell there, for the famine was severe in the land. And it came to pass, when he was close to entering Egypt, that he said to Sarai his wife, 'Indeed I know that you are a woman of beautiful countenance. Therefore it will happen, when the Egyptians see you, that they will say, 'This is his wife'; and they will kill me, but they will let you live. Please say you are my sister, that it may be well with me for your sake, and that I may live because of you.' So it was, when Abram came into Egypt, that the Egyptians saw the woman, that she was very beautiful. The princes of Pharaoh also saw her and commended her to Pharaoh. And the woman was taken to Pharaoh's house. He treated Abram well for her sake. He had sheep, oxen, male donkeys, male and female servants, female donkeys, and camels. But the LORD plagued Pharaoh and his house with great plagues because of Sarai, Abram's wife.*

*And Pharaoh called Abram and said, 'What is this you*

*have done to me? Why did you not tell me that she was your wife? Why did you say, "She is my sister"? I might have taken her as my wife. Now therefore, here is your wife; take her and go your way.' So Pharaoh commanded his men concerning him; and they sent him away, with his wife and all that he had. Then Abram went up from Egypt, he and his wife and all that he had, and Lot with him, to the South"* (Genesis 12:10-13:1).

We might view this as Abram's 'trial in Egypt.' About the most helpful thing I've heard said of trials is that we don't need to fail them. That's based on 1 Corinthians 10:13 where it says: *"God is faithful, who will not allow you to be tempted beyond what you are able, but with the temptation (or trial – same word) will also make the way of escape, that you may be able to bear it."*

As Christians, we can and do fail when we don't take the way of escape God offers. As I see it, Abram attempted to work out his own deliverance here, instead of taking God's way of escape. The excursion into Egypt was a sad episode of failure in the life of this great man. We don't read of him building any altar to God there. His behaviour wasn't a good witness to God in Egypt. Perhaps that should make us pause, and think about whether we, too, have got ourselves into circumstances just now that are not making it easy for us to witness.

Eventually, Abram seems to come out of Egypt richer and wiser by the grace of God. He was wiser because, in the story that follows, we can easily detect that his faith has been revived. In this story perhaps there's another word from the Lord for some of us. Abram says to his nephew: "let there be no strife between you and me... for we are brethren." Is there someone with whom you're at odds – in your family circle perhaps, or in the Christian fellowship you're part of? Consider taking these words to heart as we go on to learn that:

> *"Abram was very rich in livestock, in silver, and in gold. And he went on his journey from the South ... to the place of the altar which he had made there at first. And there Abram called on the name of the LORD. Lot also, who went with Abram, had flocks and herds and tents. Now the land was not able to support them, that they might dwell together, for their possessions were so great that they could not dwell together. And there was strife between the herdsmen of Abram's livestock and the herdsmen of Lot's livestock ...*

> *So Abram said to Lot, 'Please let there be no strife between you and me, and between my herdsmen and your herds– men; for we are brethren. Is not the whole land before you? Please separate from me. If you take the left, then I will go to the right; or, if you go to the right, then I will go to the left.' And Lot lifted his eyes and saw all the plain of Jordan, that it was well watered everywhere (before the LORD destroyed Sodom and Gomorrah) like the garden of the LORD, like the land of Egypt as you go toward Zoar.*

> *Then Lot chose for himself all the plain of Jordan, and Lot journeyed east. And they separated from each other. Abram dwelt in the land of Canaan, and Lot dwelt in the cities of the plain and pitched his tent even as far as Sodom. But the men of Sodom were exceedingly wicked and sinful*

*against the LORD. And the LORD said to Abram, after Lot had separated from him: 'Lift your eyes now and look from the place where you are – northward, southward, eastward, and westward; for all the land which you see I give to you and your descendants forever'" (Genesis 13:2 – 15).*

We ask ourselves: what can we learn about God's purposes from Abram's experience? The first point, I think, is this: that God is sovereign. What this adventure has clearly demonstrated is that the man with the call of God, Abram, was the man without a choice! His nephew, Lot – as I understand it – didn't share in Abram's calling from God. Perhaps, it was because he'd no sense of the call of God that he appeared to have all the choice in the world. Abram, operating here within his understanding of the will of God for his life, was content to give his nephew the choice, and to leave himself with no choice.

He was someone with a deep sense of the sovereign God at the helm of his life. Was it the case, we ask, that his grasp of the call of God on his life was such that it left him realizing he'd no choice of his life? Do we feel like that about the overall way in which we serve God? After all, doesn't the apostle Peter talks about making *"our calling and election sure"* (2 Peter 1)? That's us affirming God's call. Perhaps, then, it would be good to ask ourselves: Is the strength of my conviction about God's call such that I don't believe I have a choice about which church I should join? Instead, is it my conviction that the choice is God's – and that his will for me in the matter is set out in his Word?

Another thing we'll come to appreciate about God's purposes –

as we glimpse them in the case of Abraham – is that they often start out small. God may begin with a single individual, but all the while he had the future service of Israel collectively in view. God's purposes may start small like a river but they widen out as they flow on through time. Another point, I suggest, is that God's purposes demand of us – as they certainly did of Abram – an uncompromising and radical response. This brings in the matter of faith and obedience, so well modelled by Abram.

One last observation is that the revelation of God's purposes is often progressive. Remember, we described four periods in Abram's recorded life – each ushered in by a fresh advance in divine revelation. When we're newly born-again, we can't hope to know all God's will for our life of service at that point, but the Spirit of God is our guide into all the truth (John 3:16).

# 3

# ENCOUNTERS WITH KINGS

War is a subject that's never far from the news headlines today. We've grown all too familiar with 'cold war', nuclear war, guerrilla war, and war on terrorism. Two thousand years ago, Jesus Christ predicted a time when wars and rumours of wars would be rife. In fact, about 180 million people were killed in one 20th century atrocity or another. This is a far larger number than for preceding centuries. The 20th century, far from showing any prospect that we're becoming any more civilised, was a century of war. As we continue the story of Abram, we come to the Bible's first mention of warfare. Genesis chapter fourteen opens like this:

> *"And it came to pass in the days of Amraphel king of Shinar, Arioch king of Ellasar, Chedorlaomer king of Elam, and Tidal king of nations, that they made war with Bera king of Sodom, Birsha king of Gomorrah, Shinab king of Admah, Shemeber king of Zeboiim, and the king of Bela (that is, Zoar). All these joined together in the Valley of Siddim (that is, the Salt Sea)"* (Genesis 14:1-3).

Hardly household names, but we can at least pick up on those of Sodom and Gomorrah. These were cities notorious for their sin and wickedness. The first four mentioned kings were on one side and heading up their list was Amraphel, king of Shinar. Shinar is the area of Babylonia; and it seems highly significant that the Bible's first mention of warfare is one in which a king of Babylon is prominent. For, at the other end of the Bible, in the Book of Revelation, a king of the north, Babylon, and military campaigns are again shown to be among the ingredients of this world's end-time crisis.

In this first Bible-recorded battle between Shinar's king and Sodom's king - each with their allies - it's probably not going too far to see a confrontation between corrupt, worldly religion (that of Shinar) and the wicked political life of the cities of the plain (Sodom). Corrupt religion and politics have always been a heady mix and the Book of Revelation reveals that little has changed towards the end of history. But what happened here in the time of Abram?

> *"And the king of Sodom, the king of Gomorrah, the king of Admah, the king of Zeboiim, and the king of Bela (that is, Zoar) went out and joined together in battle in the Valley of Siddim against Chedorlaomer king of Elam, Tidal king of nations, Amraphel king of Shinar, and Arioch king of Ellasar - four kings against five. Now the Valley of Siddim was full of asphalt pits; and the kings of Sodom and Gomorrah fled; some fell there, and the remainder fled to the mountains. Then they took all the goods of Sodom and Gomorrah, and all their provisions, and went their way. They also took Lot, Abram's brother's son who*

*dwelt in Sodom, and his goods, and departed" (Genesis 14:8-12).*

Lot had made his choice to live in and around the cities of the plain. The Bible lets us see the consequences of such decisions in the lives of its characters. Lot became affected by the wars of Sodom. He was caught up and swept away in this conflict. Abram wasn't. Lot had entangled himself in this world's affairs; whereas Abram had remained a separated pilgrim. Is this recorded episode with Lot not designed to teach us the same lesson that the apostle Paul later so wanted to impress upon his protégé, Timothy? "No one...entangles himself with the affairs of this life'"- if he or she wants to please the Lord." (2 Timothy 2:4) But Lot won't be left abandoned to his fate, for:

*"... one who had escaped came and told Abram the Hebrew, for he dwelt by the terebinth trees of Mamre the Amorite, brother of Eshcol and brother of Aner; and they were allies with Abram. Now when Abram heard that his brother was taken captive, he armed his three hundred and eighteen trained servants who were born in his own house, and went in pursuit as far as Dan. He divided his forces against them by night, and he and his servants attacked them and pursued them as far as Hobah, which is north of Damascus. So he brought back all the goods, and also brought back his brother Lot and his goods, as well as the women and the people" (Genesis 14:13-16).*

As well as showing us that Abram was of such standing that he could quickly muster a private army and mobilize them effectively, I suggest this incident demonstrates a spiritual truth which we come across in Galatians 6:1-2: *"If a man is overtaken in any trespass, you who are spiritual restore such a one in a spirit of gentleness, considering yourself lest you also be tempted. Bear one another's burdens, and so fulfill the law of Christ."*

In rescuing Lot from the mess he'd got himself into, Abraham was certainly making concern for Lot his own personal concern. There's no hint later of any finger-wagging: 'I told you this would happen!' Abram acts graciously out of sincere compassion for his nephew Lot. But things are happening fast. Abram is about to receive two visitors. Here they come:

> *"And the king of Sodom went out to meet him at the Valley of Shaveh (that is, the King's Valley), after his return from the defeat of Chedorlaomer and the kings who were with him. Then Melchizedek king of Salem brought out bread and wine; he was the priest of God Most High. And he blessed him and said: 'Blessed be Abram of God Most High, Possessor of heaven and earth; and blessed be God Most High, who has delivered your enemies into your hand'. And he gave him a tithe of all. Now the king of Sodom said to Abram, 'Give me the persons, and take the goods for yourself.' But Abram said to the king of Sodom, 'I have raised my hand to the LORD, God Most High, the Possessor of heaven and earth, that I will take nothing, from a thread to a sandal strap, and that I will not take anything that is yours, lest you should say, 'I have made Abram rich'"* (Genesis 14:17-23).

The King of Babylon and the priest Melchizedek were Abram's two visitors that day. It's as if this priestly figure Melchizedek

- presented in such a way as to give us a picture of Jesus - intercepts Abram as he returns flushed with the success of victory. In human experience, is it not true that we're often most vulnerable after we've savoured some success? Mechizedek's arrival was to prove timely, strengthening Abram before the tempting offer that the king of Sodom was coming to make him. An earthly king was coming to offer Abram worldly possessions; but God's priest came pronouncing blessings from the God of heaven above. In our case it's wonderful to know that in any time of our need, we have access to a high priest where heaven's throne is. He's sympathetic too, for the Bible says:

> *"We do not have a High Priest who cannot sympathize with our weaknesses, but was in all points tempted as we are, yet without sin. Let us therefore come boldly to the throne of grace, that we may obtain mercy and find grace to help in time of need"* (Hebrews 4:15-16).

The world - just like the king of Sodom - flatters with its congratulations and honours; but true blessing comes from the Lord. It's to him that all glory is due. If Lot knew about the visit of Melchizedek, he certainly didn't take this warning, nor was he impressed with Melchizedek. There was a limit to what Lot and Abram shared in common. There was agreement inasmuch as Lot's enemies were also Abram's enemies; but Lot could not agree with Abram in refusing the king of Sodom's patronage. Lot had made his choice earlier. I would think that here was an opportunity for him to re-evaluate his choice. He didn't.

So this episode brings a double defeat for Lot because he re-affirmed his earlier worldly choice. He didn't learn, and later he's going to lose all his newly recovered goods when the city of Sodom goes up in flames. It's a searching question for us to reflect on where our wealth is. All that's down here, we must one day leave behind.  In contrast, we've witnessed a double victory for Abram - as, for the second time, he turns his back on the wealth of the cities of the Plain. God is the reward of the man of faith.

4

# ABRAHAM'S FAITH & ISRAEL'S FUTURE

Abram wouldn't have been human if he wasn't afraid of some reprisal after he'd defeated the kings. Perhaps, having declined the King of Sodom's offer to make him a rich man, there would have been at least the potential for regret in a weaker moment. So it was especially timely when: *"... after these things the word of the LORD came to Abram in a vision, saying, "Do not be afraid, Abram. I am your shield, your exceedingly great reward"'* (Genesis 15:1).

The knowledge that God was his shield would fortify him against any thought that there might be a reprisal; and the reassurance that God himself was Abram's reward would raise his sights above the kind of riches that can be measured in terms of this world's goods. After all, Abram possessed the promises of God. The most tangible sign of these promises for which Abram waited was the birth of a son and heir. He was still waiting, of course, and so took the opportunity to raise the subject with God: *'"Lord GOD, what will You give me, seeing I go childless, and the heir of my house is Eliezer of Damascus?" Then Abram said, 'Look, You have given me no offspring; indeed one born in my house is my heir!'"* (Genesis 15:2,3).

Even men of faith have a tendency to rationalize the word of God and try to understand it in human terms. Abram was already an old man - and his wife was barren. Surely some kind of adopted heir was the most likely explanation for this mysterious promise of a son. But God was clear in his reply:

> *'"This one shall not be your heir, but one who will come from your own body shall be your heir.' Then He brought him outside and said, 'Look now toward heaven, and count the stars if you are able to number them.' And He said to him, 'So shall your descendants be.' And he believed in the LORD, and He accounted it to him for righteousness"* (Genesis 15:4-6).

How wonderfully Abram's faith rose to the challenge! He believed in the LORD. And God accounted it to him for righteousness. God credited him with righteousness on account of his faith. This is the first mention in the Bible of justification by faith. To his believing friends in Rome, the apostle Paul says (4:3-5): "For what does the Scripture say? *"Abraham believed God, and it was accounted to him for righteousness." Now to him who works, the wages are not counted as grace but as debt. But to him who does not work but believes on Him who justifies the ungodly, his faith is accounted for righteousness."*

It's a teaching that was virtually lost throughout the Dark Ages and for well over a thousand years in total. Justification by faith is the glorious truth that we cannot contribute any work of our own towards procuring our salvation; we must only embrace it as a gift in simple personal faith - just as Abram in faith took God at his word. Again Paul reminds the Galatians (3:8-11):

*"And the Scripture, foreseeing that God would justify the Gentiles by faith, preached the gospel to Abraham beforehand, saying, 'In you all the nations shall be blessed.' So then those who are of faith are blessed with believing Abraham. For as many as are of the works of the law are under the curse; for it is written, 'Cursed is everyone who does not continue in all things which are written in the book of the law, to do them.' But that no one is justified by the law in the sight of God is evident, for 'the just shall live by faith.'"*

This is something the New Testament points back to time and time again. James says (2:23): "And the Scripture was fulfilled which says, *"Abraham believed God, and it was accounted to him for righteousness."* How wonderful it is to realize that we are made right with God, purely through faith on the basis of God's free grace! However, let's get back to the story-line with Abram. God is still speaking:

*"'I am the LORD, who brought you out of Ur of the Chaldeans, to give you this land to inherit it.' And he said, 'Lord GOD, how shall I know that I will inherit it?' So He said to him, 'Bring Me a three-year-old heifer, a three-year-old female goat, a three-year-old ram, a turtledove, and a young pigeon.' Then he brought all these to Him and cut them in two, down the middle, and placed each*

*piece opposite the other; but he did not cut the birds in two. And when the vultures came down on the carcasses, Abram drove them away.*

*Now when the sun was going down, a deep sleep fell upon Abram; and behold, horror and great darkness fell upon him. Then He said to Abram: 'Know certainly that your descendants will be strangers in a land that is not theirs, and will serve them, and they will afflict them four hundred years. And also the nation whom they serve I will judge; afterward they shall come out with great possessions. Now as for you, you shall go to your fathers in peace; you shall be buried at a good old age. But in the fourth generation they shall return here, for the iniquity of the Amorites is not yet complete.' And it came to pass, when the sun went down and it was dark, that behold, there appeared a smoking oven and a burning torch that passed between those pieces. On the same day the LORD made a covenant with Abram, saying: 'To your descendants I have given this land'"* (Genesis 15:7–18).

Abram sat all day waiting for God to act; awaiting God's time for anything can be difficult. Abram had to drive the birds of prey away. Maybe sometimes as we wait on God we have to drive away thoughts which prey on our minds and detract us from waiting on God. Then at sunset, Abram sank into a deep sleep in which God brought to him a nightmarish preview of the experience that would later belong to his descendants in the land of Egypt. Then, at darkest moment, God spoke. Does that ring bells for you? In the darkest hour of some experience, God has spoken to you too. He knows our limits when allowing our faith to be tested (1 Corinthians 10:13).

Then there's this business of the smoking furnace and the burning torch - obviously a symbol of God's presence - which passed between the pieces of the covenant sacrifices. In those days it was a custom between covenantees to divide a sacrifice and pass between its pieces. If either party broke the agreement, perhaps they were saying 'let me become as this animal, cut in two'. If you're in the furnace of affliction right now, remember the symbol of the burning torch here: the symbol of promised divine presence in your hour of trial. God is for us; for the deep sleep and horror of darkness here takes us in thought to the cross. Praise God that through that death has come about a greater exodus for all believers. There's an ongoing significance to all of this, for:

> *"the Scripture foreseeing that God would justify the Gentiles by faith, preached the gospel to Abraham beforehand, saying, 'In you all the nations shall be blessed.' Christ has redeemed us ... that the blessing of Abraham might come upon the Gentiles in Christ Jesus, that we might receive the promise of the Spirit through faith. 'Now to Abraham and his Seed were the promises made. He does not say, "And to seeds," as of many, but as of one, "And to your Seed," who is Christ ... For if the inheritance is of the law, it is no longer of promise; but God gave it to Abraham by promise ... But the Scripture has confined all under sin, that the promise by faith in Jesus Christ might be given to those who believe ... and if you are Christ's, then you are Abraham's seed, and heirs according to the promise"* (Galatians 3:8,13-14,16,18,22,29).

The blessing and inheritance that are ours today - through faith in Christ - are ours in accordance with the promise God made with Abram. Those of us who are justified by our faith in Jesus Christ, the Son of God, can rejoice that Abram's God is also our shield and our exceedingly great reward.

# 5

# HAGAR & ISHMAEL

Some people have written books about angels. It's a fascinating study to draw upon the Bible information on this topic which has long captivated the human mind. Our incident from the life of Abram today brings us to the first Bible mention of angels. Here's how it came about:

> *"Now Sarai, Abram's wife, had borne him no children. And she had an Egyptian maidservant whose name was Hagar. So Sarai said to Abram, 'See now, the LORD has restrained me from bearing children. Please, go in to my maid; perhaps I shall obtain children by her.' And Abram heeded the voice of Sarai. Then Sarai, Abram's wife, took Hagar her maid, the Egyptian, and gave her to her husband Abram to be his wife, after Abram had dwelt ten years in the land of Canaan. So he went in to Hagar, and she conceived"* (Genesis 16:1-4).

It's all too easy to criticize Abram for his actions here. Apart from the cultural thing of a man taking secondary wives at that time, Abram is often criticised for trying to make God's promise of a son come true. God had promised that Abram would have descendants, and while Abram should have maintained that promise, it perhaps wasn't altogether clear to him that the fulfilment of this promise was to be the result of his own personal offspring. Maybe that only became clearer as time went by. It does read as though this was something of a progressive revelation to Abram. Starting in chapter 12, God had said that Abram's descendants would become a great nation. But it wasn't until chapters 13 and 15 that God confirmed to him that his own seed was meant. It was only after this episode we're studying now - when we get to chapter 17 - that Sarai is specified as the mother-to-be. So probably things became clear very gradually to Abram as to exactly how this all-important promise was going to come true.

So before things had become clear, at Sarai's suggestion, Abram took Hagar as a second wife and she became pregnant. The story now continues and takes an unexpected twist:

> *"And when she [Hagar] saw that she had conceived, her mistress became despised in her eyes. Then Sarai said to Abram, 'My wrong be upon you! I gave my maid into your embrace; and when she saw that she had conceived, I became despised in her eyes. The LORD judge between you and me.' So Abram said to Sarai, 'Indeed your maid is in your hand; do to her as you please.' And when Sarai dealt harshly with her, she fled from her presence. Now the Angel of the LORD found her by a spring of water in the wilderness, by the spring on the way to Shur. And He said, 'Hagar, Sarai's maid, where have you come from,*

*and where are you going?' She said, 'I am fleeing from
the presence of my mistress Sarai"' (Genesis 16:4-8).*

So here's where we get the first mention of the word 'angel', although the way it's used leads us to think this visitor was more than an angel. The angel of the LORD directs two questions to this expectant mum out there in the desert. He asks her: 'Where have you come from, and where are you going?' Presumably Hagar had no idea where she was going: she was just running away from her problems. Understandable of course; Sarai hadn't left her much option really. I wonder how many of us can catch a reflection of ourselves in this? So many people rush around today, but do they really know where they're going? We're reminded of the captain of the aeroplane who tells his passengers he has both good and bad news for them. The good news is they're making excellent progress. The bad news is they've no idea in which direction they're headed! It's hardly funny when you think there are so many people like this - when viewed from the perspective of eternity.

The Lord Jesus, by contrast, told the Jews one day that he knew where he'd come from and where he was going. His words quoted from John chapter 8 capture this point: *'"My witness is true, for I know where I came from and where I am going; but you do not know where I come from and where I am going.' Then Jesus said to them again, 'I am going away, and you will seek Me, and will die in your sin. Where I go you cannot come"'* (John 8:14,21). In contrast to those disbelieving Jews, believers on Jesus who follow him as his disciples, know where they're going; they are going to be with Jesus. That was his promise in John 14:

*"'And if I go and prepare a place for you, I will come again and receive you to Myself; that where I am, there you may be also. And where I go you know, and the way you know.' Thomas said to Him, 'Lord, we do not know where You are going, and how can we know the way?' Jesus said to him, 'I am the way, the truth, and the life. No one comes to the Father except through Me'"* (John 14:3–6).

Back in the time of Abram, it was when Hagar was out alone in the desert that she really discovered that she had no place to go. It was when she acknowledged this that she 'found God'. For God sent his angel who said: "Return to your mistress, and submit yourself under her hand." It's never good to run away from our problems. It's always better to submit to God's will even in difficult circumstances - and they don't come much more desperate than Hagar's. Yet God gave her good reason to hope, for his message to her was:

*"'I will multiply your descendants exceedingly, so that they shall not be counted for multitude.' And the Angel of the LORD said to her: 'Behold, you are with child, and you shall bear a son. You shall call his name Ishmael, because the LORD has heard your affliction. He shall be a wild man; his hand shall be against every man, and every man's hand against him. And he shall dwell in the presence of all his brethren'"* (Genesis 16:10–12).

When we read these words about this son of Abraham who would become the father of the Arab nations - and that he was to be anything but a son of peace - is it any wonder that peace seems to be beyond reach in the Middle East today?

*"Then she [Hagar] called the name of the LORD who spoke to her, You-Are-the-God-Who-Sees; for she said, "Have I also here seen Him who sees me?" So Hagar bore Abram a son; and Abram named his son, whom Hagar bore, Ishmael. Abram was eighty-six years old when Hagar bore Ishmael to Abram"* (Genesis 16:13-16).

When the New Testament comments on this episode in Galatians chapter 4, it calls Isaac - not Ishmael - the 'son of promise'. Ishmael was born of the flesh. In other words, his birth was the result of Abram trying to please God by his own human efforts. The big lesson for us is surely this: it's hopeless for us to think we can help forward God's promise in our own strength. What God called Abram to believe was to be fully revealed as something that was - humanly speaking - impossible of fulfilment. That's meant to make us think of the Gospel in which we're called to believe, is it not? God's Good News of us being able to have our sins forgiven and receiving a righteousness that meets God's standard is an impossibility we're called upon to believe.

It's an impossibility as far as we and our own abilities to achieve it are concerned. But, as Jesus said to the disciples one day, *"The things which are impossible with men are possible with God"* (Luke 18:27). Let's not put any confidence in our best human attempts to earn salvation. We need to leave the impossible to God. For, *"to Him* [that's Jesus] *all the prophets witness that, through His name, whoever believes in Him will receive remission of sins"* (Acts 10:43).

6

# GOD'S COVENANT & ITS SEAL

Earlier in this book, we noted that the life of Abram, as recorded in the Bible, can be divided into four stages - each of them starting with a special revelation from God. First, there was his call and removal to Haran at the very beginning of the story, as told in Genesis chapter 12. Then there was the time he received from God the promise of a son and heir (Genesis 15) when God made a covenant with him there. Now we've reached the third stage in Abram's life - one which again begins with him having an encounter with the living God:

> *"When Abram was ninety-nine years old, the LORD appeared to Abram and said to him, 'I am Almighty God; walk before Me and be blameless. And I will make My covenant between Me and you, and will multiply you exceedingly.' Then Abram fell on his face ..."* (Genesis 17:1-3).

It was to prove to be an encounter in which God would change his name from Abram to Abraham. At this time God also renews his covenant with him, and gives him the token of circumcision - as we see, for:

> *"God talked with him, saying: 'As for Me, behold, My covenant is with you, and you shall be a father of many nations. No longer shall your name be called Abram, but your name shall be Abraham; for I have made you a father of many nations. I will make you exceedingly fruitful; and I will make nations of you, and kings shall come from you. And I will establish My covenant between Me and you and your descendants after you in their generations, for an everlasting covenant, to be God to you and your descendants after you. Also I give to you and your descendants after you the land in which you are a stranger, all the land of Canaan, as an everlasting possession; and I will be their God.'*
>
> *And God said to Abraham: "As for you, you shall keep My covenant, you and your descendants after you throughout their generations. This is My covenant which you shall keep, between Me and you and your descendants after you: every male child among you shall be circumcised; and you shall be circumcised in the flesh of your foreskins, and it shall be a sign of the covenant between Me and you"'* (Genesis 17:3-11).

So God renewed the basic elements of the covenant he'd previously made with Abram in chapter 15. He now establishes the covenant - and goes on to develop Abraham's responsibilities in answering to it. He commands Abraham to "walk before Me and be blameless". The emphasis on 'walk' and 'be blameless' introduces the obligation of obedience.

This renewal of the Genesis 15 covenant also introduces the fact that the covenant is to be sealed by the token or sign of circumcision. About two thousand years later, in the early days of Christianity, this matter of circumcision would cause some problems. This was because the first Christians were Jews, and some thought circumcision was an essential ingredient that counted towards their salvation. Circumcision, however, was never taught as necessary for salvation. No-one made the case clearer than Paul when writing to Christian disciples at Rome. He asks in chapter 4:

> *"What does the Scripture say? 'Abraham believed God, and it was accounted to him for righteousness' … blessed is the man to whom the Lord shall not impute sin. Does this blessedness then come upon the circumcised only, or upon the uncircumcised also? For we say that faith was accounted to Abraham for righteousness. How then was it accounted? While he was circumcised, or uncircumcised? Not while circumcised, but while uncircumcised.*

> *And he received the sign of circumcision, a seal of the righteousness of the faith which he had while still uncircumcised, that he might be the father of all those who believe, though they are uncircumcised, that righteousness might be imputed to them also, and the father of circumcision to those who not only are of the circumcision, but who also walk in the steps of the faith which our father Abraham had while still uncircumcised"* (Romans 4:3,8-12).

I doubt whether Paul could have made it clearer. God credited Abraham with righteousness. In other words, God cleared him of the guilt of sin - on the basis of the faith he had while still uncircumcised. Circumcision was never necessary for salvation. So Paul had this to say to Galatian believers because there were some who wanted Christians to be circumcised in those early days of Christianity. He spoke of them as those who want:

> *"... to make a good showing in the flesh, these would compel you to be circumcised, only that they may not suffer persecution for the cross of Christ. For not even those who are circumcised keep the law, but they desire to have you circumcised that they may boast in your flesh. But God forbid that I should boast except in the cross of our Lord Jesus Christ, by whom the world has been crucified to me, and I to the world. For in Christ Jesus neither circumcision nor uncircumcision avails anything, but a new creation"* (Galatians 6:12-15).

As a once proud Pharisee, Paul had boasted of his circumcised status; but he boasted in it no longer. All he boasted in now was the cross of Christ. Actually, the Bible describes our spiritual condition before we receive Jesus Christ in personal faith for salvation as being the spiritual equivalent of being 'uncircumcised' (see Colossians 2:13). Spiritually, that condition is changed when we become a son of Abraham through faith in Abraham's 'seed' - that being a reference to Christ in Galatians 3:16. That takes us back to Abraham, and his faith, which was still being tested in Genesis chapter 17:

> *"Then God said to Abraham, 'As for Sarai your wife, you*

*shall not call her name Sarai, but Sarah shall be her name. And I will bless her and also give you a son by her; then I will bless her, and she shall be a mother of nations; kings of peoples shall be from her.' Then Abraham fell on his face and laughed, and said in his heart, 'Shall a child be born to a man who is one hundred years old? And shall Sarah, who is ninety years old, bear a child?' And Abraham said to God, 'Oh, that Ishmael might live before You!' Then God said: 'No, Sarah your wife shall bear you a son, and you shall call his name Isaac; I will establish My covenant with him for an everlasting covenant, and with his descendants after him ... But My covenant I will establish with Isaac, whom Sarah shall bear to you at this set time next year'"* (Genesis 17:15–21).

This is the first time that God really makes it clear to Abraham that Sarah his wife is to be the mother of his long-promised son and heir. There would be no question of his adopting a son and heir, or hoping that the son of a secondary wife would be acceptable. Abraham is recorded here as laughing when God spelt this out, but the New Testament explains this was not incredulous laughter, for it says:

*"Abraham ... in hope believed, so that he became the father of many nations, according to what was spoken, 'So shall your descendants be.' And not being weak in faith, he did not consider his own body, already dead (since he was about a hundred years old), and the deadness of Sarah's womb. He did not waver at the promise of God through unbelief, but was strengthened in faith, giving glory to God, and being fully convinced that what He had*

*promised He was also able to perform. And therefore 'it was accounted to him for righteousness.' Now it was not written for his sake alone that it was imputed to him, but also for us. It shall be imputed to us who believe in Him who raised up Jesus our Lord from the dead, who was delivered up because of our offenses, and was raised because of our justification"* (Romans 4:16–25).

This is the Good News: that we, too, can be right with God by simply believing in what God has done for us through Jesus Christ and his death on the cross for our sins. This chapter, Genesis 17, therefore has great importance for all who are Abraham's seed, whether through Isaac or Christ. The promise given to Abraham concerning the land remains, as does God's place for Abraham's natural seed through Isaac, but Galatians chapter 3 shows us that the promises reach much further, embracing the salvation of all Christian believers, with Abraham's seed taken as indicating Christ.

# 7

# THE DAY IT RAINED FIRE

The Bible teaches us so many things by allowing us to observe the lives of men and women and, in particular, their dealings with God. We get to see the impact of their decisions as we trace consequences they had to live with for years afterwards. We've already seen the contrasting choices of Abraham and his nephew Lot. As the story now moves into Genesis chapter 18 we again find Abraham and Lot brought together in contrasting lights. This enables us to see further the impact of their respective choices.

Years before, Lot had chosen the watered plains of the Jordan River and had become a city-dweller in Sodom; whereas Abraham had continued to have a nomadic type existence in the land which God had promised to his descendants. He lived separate from sophisticated city-life in a lifestyle marked out by the stark simplicity of his tent and altar and experiences of the presence of God. Here's another of those we read about in Genesis 18: "Then the LORD appeared to him by the terebinth trees of Mamre, as he was sitting in the tent door in the heat of the day ... And the LORD said, 'Shall I hide from Abraham what I am doing?'" (Genesis 18:1,17).

Abraham had known association with the altar at Mamre for many years.  His experience of God had grown deeper in the fullness of that separated lifestyle. So it's no surprise that we find him being favoured with intimacy in divine secrets – "for the secret of the Lord is with them that fear him", the psalmist said (Psalm 25:4).

> *"And the LORD said, 'Because the outcry against Sodom and Gomorrah is great, and because their sin is very grave, I will go down now and see whether they have done altogether according to the outcry against it that has come to Me; and if not, I will know.' And Abraham came near and said, 'Would You also destroy the righteous with the wicked?  Suppose there were fifty righteous within the city; would You also destroy the place and not spare it for the fifty righteous that were in it? Far be it from You to do such a thing as this, to slay the righteous with the wicked, so that the righteous should be as the wicked; far be it from You! Shall not the Judge of all the earth do right?' So the LORD said, 'If I find in Sodom fifty righteous within the city, then I will spare all the place for their sakes.' Then Abraham answered and said, 'Indeed now, I who am but dust and ashes have taken it upon myself to speak to the Lord: Suppose there were five less than the fifty righteous; would You destroy all of the city for lack of five?'*
>
> *So He said, 'If I find there forty-five, I will not destroy it.' And he spoke to Him yet again and said, 'Suppose there*

*should be forty found there?' So He said, 'I will not do it for the sake of forty.' Then he said, 'Let not the Lord be angry, and I will speak: Suppose thirty should be found there?' So He said, 'I will not do it if I find thirty there.' And he said, 'Indeed now, I have taken it upon myself to speak to the Lord: Suppose twenty should be found there?' So He said, 'I will not destroy it for the sake of twenty.' Then he said, 'Let not the Lord be angry, and I will speak but once more: Suppose ten should be found there?' And He said, 'I will not destroy it for the sake of ten.' So the LORD went His way as soon as He had finished speaking with Abraham; and Abraham returned to his place"* (Genesis 18:20-33).

Abraham is very conscious of the boldness of his praying. He knows, of course, that his own nephew is down there among the places that are shortly to be destroyed, yet he leaves Lot unnamed in his intercession. Let's draw near with boldness to God's throne of grace as we pray - and especially as we pray for family and friends who are not going on with the Lord (Hebrews 4:15-16). The scene now switches away from Abraham's bold interceding in the separated place, to the nephew Lot himself, in the thick of the doomed city of Sodom:

*"Now the two angels came to Sodom in the evening, and Lot was sitting in the gate of Sodom. When Lot saw them, he rose to meet them, and he bowed himself with his face toward the ground ...Then the men said to Lot, 'Have you anyone else here? Son-in-law, your sons, your daughters, and whomever you have in the city - take them out of this place!'"* (Genesis 19:1,12).

Lot was sitting in the gate of Sodom. In those days the city gate was the place where the city elders sat. These were the people of influence in all the affairs of the city. Our word 'politics' comes from an old word for 'city'. The gate of the city was the seat of city politics in those days. On meeting Lot, the angels asked the question: *"Have you anyone else here?"* It was a question that exposed the lack of impact Lot's witness had in that place - even among his own household. As it transpires, very few had been influenced by his righteous lifestyle. Peter in the New Testament (2 Peter 2:7-8) describes Lot as a righteous man, albeit in an unrighteous situation. I find it hard not to think of Lot as I read Paul's instructions to Timothy - that he should not be someone who *"entangles himself with the affairs of this life."*

In Lot we can see a worked example of someone who, perhaps with the sincerest motivation, entangled himself in the affairs of Sodom. As the angels continue their conversation with Lot, they say: *"We will destroy this place, because the outcry against them has grown great before the face of the LORD, and the LORD has sent us to destroy it." So Lot went out and spoke to his sons-in-law, who had married his daughters, and said, 'Get up, get out of this place; for the LORD will destroy this city!' But to his sons-in-law he seemed to be joking. When the morning dawned, the angels urged Lot to hurry, saying, 'Arise, take your wife and your two daughters who are here, lest you be consumed in the punishment of the city.' And while he lingered, the men took hold of his hand, his wife's hand, and the hands of his two daughters, the LORD being merciful to him, and they brought him out and set him outside the city."*

The Lord set Lot 'outside the city'. He's now where God wants him. Perhaps, again, we're reminded of Paul's words to

Timothy: *"Let everyone who names the name of Christ depart from iniquity"* (2 Timothy 2:19). Outside the camp, or city, is the place of separation to where the Lord is. Abraham had grasped this as part of his calling, but Lot paid the price for his involvement in Sodom. It appears to have influenced Lot and his family more than they had managed to influence it. Surely that's the danger the Bible warns us about. Lot's constrained to leave in the end, but not before his family members have been tainted by Sodom's immorality.

Lot's spirituality had declined in the traffic of the city life he'd favoured - despite the indication that he had attained to a position of some influence in the affairs of the city (19:1,9), in reality he'd achieved so little - and even that little he owed to Abraham's intercession! Lot had gone in with great possessions (Genesis 13:5) - but he came out with very few. In that sense I'm reminded of Paul's words to the Corinthians (1 Corinthians 3:11-15):

> *"No other foundation can anyone lay than that which is laid, which is Jesus Christ. Now if anyone builds on this foundation with gold, silver, precious stones, wood, hay, straw, each one's work will become clear; for the Day will declare it, because it will be revealed by fire; and the fire will test each one's work, of what sort it is. If anyone's work which he has built on it endures, he will receive a reward. If anyone's work is burned, he will suffer loss; but he himself will be saved, yet so as through fire."*

These words apply to the assessment of each believer's life when, in a coming day, we stand before Christ's judgement-seat. Will we do better than Lot?  Lot escaped then from the flames of Sodom, a righteous man, but with little or nothing to show for it.  He suffered loss while being saved. Abraham, in contrast, goes back to the place of his enriching encounter with God: *"And Abraham went early in the morning to the place where he had stood before the LORD. Then he looked toward Sodom and Gomorrah, and toward all the land of the plain; and he saw, and behold, the smoke of the land which went up like the smoke of a furnace"* (Genesis 19:27–28).

God takes no pleasure in the death of the wicked (Ezekiel 18:23, 32; 33:11), and only overthrew the cities of the plain after - in his mercy - he'd given them ample opportunity to turn from their degradation. Interestingly, in the Dead Sea area, beds of salt and gypsum are found.  In Genesis chapter 14, too, we're told that the Vale of Siddim - that's the Dead Sea area - was full of bitumen pits. Apparently, at places there are extensive salt deposits under a yellow layer - the natural home of sulphur from which the burning brimstone could easily have been used by God to destroy the cities of the plain.  Then it would have rained salt together with fire and brimstone - and any person caught up in such a cataclysm - like it says of Lot's wife - would be overcome by gases and covered by salt so as to become a pillar - just as the nearby hills are to this day covered with salt which has been precipitated on them. What a lesson! *"Remember Lot's wife,"* Jesus said.

# REAL SATISFACTION

None of us finds it easy to wait on the Lord. It's easier to try to make things happen, even things that God has promised us. In following the story of Abraham, we've seen how he has already tried to help God to deliver on his promise. It makes it easier for us to sympathize with Abraham when we remember that it has been twenty-five years since God first began to speak to him about the promise of a son. Then, after all this time, we read at last that:

> *"... the LORD visited Sarah as He had said, and the LORD did for Sarah as He had spoken. For Sarah conceived and bore Abraham a son in his old age, at the set time of which God had spoken to him. And Abraham called the name of his son who was born to him – whom Sarah bore to him – Isaac. Then Abraham circumcised his son Isaac when he was eight days old, as God had commanded him. Now Abraham was one hundred years old when his son Isaac was born to him. And Sarah said, 'God has made me laugh, and all who hear will laugh with me'"* (Genesis

21:1-6).

It's little wonder, then, that they called the baby 'laughter', which is the meaning of the name Isaac. In more ways than one, Isaac's birth proved to be a turning-point in Abraham's career. We've noted before that the Bible doesn't flatter its heroes. We've read about some of the blemishes in Abraham's life: when he went down into Egypt to escape famine and encouraged his wife Sarah to tell half-truths about being his sister. Now we find something quite interesting. After Isaac is born, there's no more mention of any failure on Abraham's part. After the birth of the son it's victory all the way, with no more recorded lapses. Maybe we can find something to think about in that. Because of the birth of Abraham's greater seed - that's Christ - we are more than conquerors through faith in Jesus. This is all due to the birth of a son: God's Son. Meanwhile, back to the story of Abraham where we find that:

*"... the child grew and was weaned. And Abraham made a great feast on the same day that Isaac was weaned. And Sarah saw the son of Hagar the Egyptian, whom she had borne to Abraham, scoffing. Therefore she said to Abraham, 'Cast out this bondwoman and her son; for the son of this bondwoman shall not be heir with my son, namely with Isaac.' And the matter was very displeasing in Abraham's sight because of his son. But God said to Abraham, 'Do not let it be displeasing in your sight because of the lad or because of your bondwoman. Whatever Sarah has said to you, listen to her voice; for in Isaac your seed shall be called. Yet I will also make a nation of the son of the bondwoman, because he is*

*your seed.' So Abraham rose early in the morning, and took bread and a skin of water; and putting it on her shoulder, he gave it and the boy to Hagar, and sent her away. Then she departed and wandered in the Wilderness of Beersheba"* (Genesis 21:8-14).

A water bottle in a desert is basically nothing, wouldn't you agree? Yet I can't help relating it to the kind of instant gratification many people go in for. God's provision for Hagar was to enable her to see a well of water. In God, we find satisfaction that lasts - compared with which all that this life offers is like a water bottle in a desert: just as short-lived and a mere dead-end. Why did Abraham - who was a rich man - give such meagre, insufficient provisions to Hagar and Ishmael when it came to the send-off? Part of the answer, I suggest, is found in the way how - later on - the Bible makes the strife between Ishmael and Isaac into a picture of something else that's a lot nearer to home for every believer on the Lord Jesus. Paul says in Galatians 5:17: *"For the flesh lusts against the Spirit, and the Spirit against the flesh; and these are contrary to one another, so that you do not do the things that you wish."*

It's in the fourth chapter of his letter to the Galatians that Paul goes on to make this picture more explicit. He's addressing Jewish Christians who were considering turning their back on Christianity and returning to Judaism - with all that meant in terms of observing the law:

*"Tell me,"* - he says - *"you who desire to be under the law, do you not hear the law? For it is written that Abraham had two sons: the one by a bondwoman, the*

*other by a freewoman. But he who was of the bondwoman was born according to the flesh, and he of the freewoman through promise, which things are symbolic. For these are the two covenants: the one from Mount Sinai which gives birth to bondage, which is Hagar – for this Hagar is Mount Sinai in Arabia, and corresponds to Jerusalem which now is, and is in bondage with her children – but the Jerusalem above is free, which is the mother of us all.*

*For it is written: 'Rejoice, O barren, you who do not bear! Break forth and shout, you who are not in labor! For the desolate has many more children than she who has a husband.' Now we, brethren, as Isaac was, are children of promise. But, as he who was born according to the flesh then persecuted him who was born according to the Spirit, even so it is now. Nevertheless what does the Scripture say? 'Cast out the bondwoman and her son, for the son of the bondwoman shall not be heir with the son of the freewoman.' So then, brethren, we are not children of the bondwoman but of the free"* (Galatians 4:21–31).

It's highly unusual (unique, in fact) for the New Testament to treat an Old Testament story in this way: making it serve as an allegory – where one subject is described under the guise of another in story form. Paul sees these two women, Hagar and Sarah, as two covenants, the Old featuring the law and Sinai and Jerusalem; and the New featuring the new birth and heaven and Jesus' teaching. Paul was saying to these backsliding Galatian believers that they were to cast out any thought of returning to the old way of the Law of Moses. It was to be cast out just as emphatically as Abraham cast out Hagar and Ishmael. Ishmael was the son born to Hagar according to the flesh in an attempt to fulfil God's promise by a human means. But Isaac was the son of promise, the seed God had promised to Abraham, the one he'd had to wait for.

For these first century Jewish believers, there was an appeal to the flesh (their basic human nature) in going back to the impressive ritual of the Law of Moses, but in language that again seems to reflect Abraham's scant provision for Hagar, Paul wrote to his Christian friends at Rome and said at the end of chapter 13: *"Put on the Lord Jesus Christ, and make no provision for the flesh, to fulfill its lusts"* (v.14).

In any case, Abraham wasn't being heartless, for he had God's promise that he would make a nation of Ishmael; so that would reassure him in the reasonableness of his action that day. I wonder if it's possible that this apparently harsh way in which Abraham treated those of his own household had prompted Abimelech to think that he'd better make an effort to secure Abraham's good graces. Because we read:

> *"... that Abimelech ... spoke to Abraham, saying, 'God is with you in all that you do. Now therefore, swear to me by God that you will not deal falsely with me, with my offspring, or with my posterity; but that according to the kindness that I have done to you, you will do to me and to the land in which you have dwelt.' And Abraham said, 'I will swear.' The two of them swore an oath there. Thus they made a covenant at Beersheba ...Then Abraham planted a tamarisk tree in Beersheba, and there called on the name of the LORD, the Everlasting God" (Genesis*

21:22-24,31-33).

So they swore an oath at the place they called the well of the oath, Beersheba. It was there Abraham planted a small tree with thick foliage and spikes of pink blooms. It was the sort of tree that would have provided ample shade for desert travellers. And so it's here we take our leave of Abraham for now: sitting under the shade of this tree and calling on the name of the everlasting God. He was there in the shadow of the presence of his God, in the secret place of the Almighty (Psalm 91:1,2). He had just sworn an oath with Abimelech. The force of the word (first used here) is that Abraham had 'sevened' himself, meaning he had given his complete commitment.

Abraham's primary commitment, however, was to his God, in whose shadow he remained. I'm sure the shade of this tree was a delightful, desert sanctuary in which Abraham communed with his God. A solitary tree in a barren land was very appropriate for a man who had grown accustomed to the barrenness and hopelessness of his own efforts, and come to rest content in the singular promises of his God.

9

# TOTAL SURRENDER

Try to imagine what it would be like if God were to ask you to give up the one thing that was most precious to you. What would it be like if you were challenged to let go of something that held the most tender association for you? One day, that became a reality for Abraham. God asked him to sacrifice his son Isaac. Forget the fact Abraham had waited 25 years for the birth of this special son; this was a request that was enough to make Abraham question everything he'd ever thought he had known about God. A human sacrifice? Had God turned into a monster? But there was no mistaking God's intention, as we read it from Genesis chapter 22:

> *"Now it came to pass after these things that God tested Abraham, and said to him, 'Abraham!' And he said, 'Here I am.' And He said, 'Take now your son, your only son Isaac, whom you love, and go to the land of Moriah, and offer him there as a burnt offering on one of the mountains of which I shall tell you"' (vv.1,2).*

Abraham must surely have wrestled in his mind with a request like this. I imagine a tortured figure on the slopes of Beersheba pouring his heart out to God to enquire if there wasn't some other thing that could be done instead. I wonder if he told God that life for him wouldn't be worth living if Isaac were dead. It can't be wrong to imagine the anguish of a distraught father, can it? Yet the Bible records no detail of any trauma. Whatever emotional struggle preceded it, Abraham got to the point where he simply believed God would bring Isaac back to life again. We know this from the New Testament commentary in Hebrews chapter 11. It seems that was the only way this man of faith could reconcile this shocking request with all he'd ever known of the character of his God - not to mention the promises for the future which were all absolutely bound up with the life of Isaac. However, the Bible story continues in a matter-of-fact type way:

*"So Abraham rose early in the morning and saddled his donkey, and took two of his young men with him, and Isaac his son; and he split the wood for the burnt offering, and arose and went to the place of which God had told him. Abraham took the wood of the burnt offering and laid it on Isaac his son; and he took the fire in his hand, and a knife, and the two of them went together. But Isaac spoke to Abraham his father and said, 'My father!'*

*And he said, 'Here I am, my son.' Then he said, 'Look, the fire and the wood, but where is the lamb for a burnt offering?' And Abraham said, 'My son, God will provide for Himself the lamb for a burnt offering.' So the two of them went together. Then they came to the place of which*

*God had told him. And Abraham built an altar there and placed the wood in order; and he bound Isaac his son and laid him on the altar, upon the wood. And Abraham stretched out his hand and took the knife to slay his son.*

*But the Angel of the LORD called to him from heaven and said, 'Abraham, Abraham!' And he said, 'Here I am.' And He said, 'Do not lay your hand on the lad, or do anything to him; for now I know that you fear God, since you have not withheld your son, your only son, from Me.' Then Abraham lifted his eyes and looked, and there behind him was a ram caught in a thicket by its horns. So Abraham went and took the ram, and offered it up for a burnt offering instead of his son'* (Genesis 22:3–13).

The apostle James in his Bible letter refers to this event in the life of Abraham when he asks the question:

*"Was not Abraham our father justified by works when he offered Isaac his son on the altar? Do you see that faith was working together with his works, and by works faith was made perfect? And the Scripture was fulfilled which says, 'Abraham believed God, and it was accounted to him for righteousness.' And he was called the friend of God"* (James 2:21–23).

James' point is that real faith - as opposed to a mere profession of faith - will always have some evidence of works connected with it. Abraham is the classic example he quotes. He reminds us, *"Abraham believed God, and it was accounted to him for righteousness."* He is quoting from Genesis chapter 15 where we learn that Abraham was justified before God by his faith. But he also tells us that Abraham was justified by works when he offered Isaac in Genesis chapter 22. So we see that faith came first, and it led to works which justified Abraham in the sight of men and women. No doubt it was a very relieved Abraham who:

> *"... called the name of the place, THE-LORD-WILL-PROVIDE; as it is said to this day, 'In the Mount of The LORD it shall be provided.' Then the Angel of the LORD called to Abraham a second time out of heaven, and said: 'By Myself I have sworn, says the LORD, because you have done this thing, and have not withheld your son, your only son – blessing I will bless you, and in multiplying I will multiply your descendants as the stars of the heaven and as the sand which is on the seashore; and your descendants shall possess the gate of their enemies. In your seed all the nations of the earth shall be blessed, because you have obeyed My voice.' So Abraham returned to his young men, and they rose and went together to Beersheba; and Abraham dwelt at Beersheba"* (Genesis 22:14-19).

So Abraham went back to where he'd planted a tree in what was perhaps an otherwise featureless landscape at Beersheba. He returned with the ringing confirmation of God's promise: *"By Myself I have sworn, says the LORD, because you have done this thing, and have not withheld your son, your only son – blessing I will bless you."* What wonderful grace this shows on God's part. He never needs to confirm his word, since the word of God cannot be broken. But for our sakes, he adds his confirmation. And the promise is for us: it is for the strong encouragement of all believers who are spiritual descendants of Abraham through Christ (the seed of Galatians 3).

This is the first time in the Bible we read of God swearing an oath like this. The word 'to swear' is the word 'to seven'; so God was, in effect, sevening himself - perhaps so as to signal complete confirmation. The Holy Spirit picks up on this incident in Hebrews chapter 6 verse 19 and applies it to us today, so that we might have complete assurance that the people of God today can enter into God's immediate presence. The letter to the Hebrews very preciously talks to us about the high priestly hope of access into heaven now. Just as Abraham went back to a solitary tree in a barren landscape, so for us God's sure promises stand out starkly against the texture of the uncertain times we live in.

These promises are bound up with Jesus Christ - the seed of Abraham. Jesus Christ is not only Saviour, but also High Priest above. It's interesting that it was a ram that God provided there as a substitute for Isaac on Mount Moriah. Abraham and Isaac had talked about the need for a lamb; but what they eventually got was a ram. This is the very animal in the Bible that has a connection with priests, since a ram had to be offered in the consecration ritual for a priest (Leviticus 8).

This ram-for-lamb switch is interesting because of the fact that Jesus died as the Lamb of God to take away the sin of the world; but he rose again to serve in resurrection as the high priest in heaven, and to bring a spiritual people in to worship God. He was sworn in as priest by the word of an oath in resurrection. Of course, that was after the terrible reality of death on the cross

- just as God had sworn an oath after the symbolic death and resurrection of Isaac. The surrender of the long-promised son, and the anguish of the father seen in the story of Abraham and Isaac, poignantly anticipated the infinitely deeper crisis of the Son's death on the cross as our Substitute. The God, who may ask us to surrender whatever we most treasure, is the God who gave his own treasured Son for us.

# 10

# A BRIDE FOR THE SON

After Jesus' death on the cross, the next major event in God's plan following the resurrection was the coming of the Holy Spirit at Pentecost, as recorded in Acts chapter 2. Ever since that time the Holy Spirit has been in the world in the lives of believers. Through them - by their preaching - he's been active in spreading the good news of the forgiveness that's to be found in God's Son, Jesus Christ. One way of describing this present, on-going activity of the Spirit of God in the world is to say that He's searching for Christ's 'Bride'. This is because the Bible teaches that each and every believer, at the point of receiving forgiveness (which is when they trust Christ for salvation), becomes a child of God and a member of Christ's Church (Matthew 16:18; Ephesians 1:21-22).

This Church, many Christians agree, is also referred to as the Bride of Christ (see Ephesians 5; Revelation 19). Through the witness of Christians, the Holy Spirit is, in effect, seeking for the Bride of Christ. At the close of this day of grace, when the Church is complete, Christ will come and take it home to himself.

Some Bible-lovers have enjoyed making a link between these thoughts and the story-line of Genesis chapters 22 to 24. In chapter 22, we have Abraham surrendering his son - a parable of death and resurrection. Compare that with the death and resurrection of Jesus. Then in the next chapter we have recorded for us the death of Sarah, Abraham's wife. Compare that with the fact that, after the cross, God set aside Israel nationally in his plans.

Then in Genesis chapter 24 Abraham's servant is sent out to search for a bride for Abraham's son, Isaac. Compare that with the Spirit's work today in seeking a bride for Christ. Let's read a little background from that story of Abraham's servant being sent out to find a bride for his son. These were days of arranged marriages, as still occurs in some parts of the world today, so we read that when:

*"Abraham was old, well advanced in age; and the LORD had blessed Abraham in all things. So Abraham said to the oldest servant of his house, who ruled over all that he had, 'Please, put your hand under my thigh, and I will make you swear by the LORD, the God of heaven and the God of the earth, that you will not take a wife for my son from the daughters of the Canaanites, among whom I dwell; but you shall go to my country and to my family, and take a wife for my son Isaac.' And the servant said to him, 'Perhaps the woman will not be willing to follow me to this land. Must I take your son back to the land from which you came?' But Abraham said to him, 'Beware that you do not take my son back there. The LORD God of heaven, who took me from my father's house and from*

*the land of my family, and who spoke to me and swore to me, saying, 'To your descendants I give this land,' He will send His angel before you, and you shall take a wife for my son from there. And if the woman is not willing to follow you, then you will be released from this oath; only do not take my son back there"* (Genesis 24:1-8).

On no account did Abraham want his son's wife to be from the Canaanites, renowned as they were for their hideous pagan practices which were an offence to God. Even though Abraham's relatives, to whom the servant was directed, had become tainted with idolatry themselves, the knowledge of the true God had not died out completely among them. Abraham's servant then asks if he may take Isaac to Mesopotamia if the girl should wish to stay there. "Absolutely not!" Abraham says. He knew God had a special calling for his descendants. God had promised the land of Canaan to them. There could be no turning back. In a similar way, a Christian is taught by the Bible to look for a partner who's prepared to follow with us in our calling, and share totally in our understanding of the Lord's will.

Marriage for the Christian is to be "in the Lord" (1 Corinthians 7:39). That will involve being subject to the Lord's will. The choice of a life-partner is to be governed by our allegiance to the Lord as well as by natural affection. This will mean that if we've come to a settled conviction about serving God in a way that is in accordance with Scripture and one which, as we see it, fully owns the Lordship of Christ, then we'll surely want to seek a partner who's not only a believer, but who will walk the same way and not take us to 'another land', so to speak. Abraham's servant located Rebekah, and we'll eavesdrop when he's at the point of telling the prospective bride's parents how he came to find her:

> *"And this day I came to the well and said, 'O LORD God of my master Abraham, if You will now prosper the way in which I go, behold, I stand by the well of water; and it shall come to pass that when the virgin comes out to draw water, and I say to her, "Please give me a little water from your pitcher to drink," and she says to me, "Drink, and I will draw for your camels also," – let her be the woman whom the LORD has appointed for my master's son.' But before I had finished speaking in my heart, there was Rebekah, coming out with her pitcher on her shoulder; and she went down to the well and drew water. And I said to her, 'Please let me drink.' And she made haste and let her pitcher down from her shoulder, and said, 'Drink, and I will give your camels a drink also.' So I drank, and she gave the camels a drink also.*

> *Then I asked her, and said, 'Whose daughter are you?' And she said, 'The daughter of Bethuel, Nahor's son, whom Milcah bore to him.' ... And I bowed my head and worshiped the LORD, and blessed the LORD God of my master Abraham, who had led me in the way of truth to take the daughter of my master's brother for his son ... 'Then the servant brought out jewelry of silver, jewelry of gold, and clothing, and gave them to Rebekah. He also gave precious things to her brother and to her mother."*

In any matter of guidance – including marriage guidance – it's of first importance that we make it a matter of prayer, as

Abraham's servant did here. Let's just share one other point. Remember how earlier we were suggesting how it's possible to see a parallel between the servant seeking a bride for Isaac, on the one hand; and the Holy Spirit today seeking a bride for Christ, God's Son, on the other hand?

That Bride we described as the Church, Christ's Church - all who belong to him by their faith in him as Saviour. In terms of that comparison, maybe we can picture the Holy Spirit today taking of the things of Christ and sharing them with us, as we read here of the servant's action in giving to Rebekah the precious gold and silver things he had brought. It's said of the Holy Spirit in John 16:14 that his ministry would glorify Christ. He would take of the things of Christ and disclose them to us as believers.

How preciously true that is - as through the reading of our Bibles, the Spirit shows us fresh glories of the person of God's Son! But let's return and finish off our story for today - for we haven't yet said if Rebekah accepted this arrangement:

> "*Then Rebekah and her maids arose, and they rode on the camels and followed the man. So the servant took Rebekah and departed. Now Isaac came from the way of Beer Lahai Roi, for he dwelt in the South. And Isaac went out to meditate in the field in the evening; and he lifted his eyes and looked, and there, the camels were coming. Then Rebekah lifted her eyes, and when she saw Isaac she dismounted from her camel; for she had said to the servant, 'Who is this man walking in the field to meet us?' And the servant said, 'It is my master.' So she took a veil and covered herself. And the servant told Isaac*

*all the things that he had done. Then Isaac brought her into his mother Sarah's tent; and he took Rebekah and she became his wife, and he loved her. So Isaac was comforted after his mother's death"* (Genesis 24:61-67).

Let's note some further resemblances between this first meeting of Rebekah and Isaac and our own spiritual experience as we journey to meet our Lord and Lover. As Rebekah journeyed on to meet Isaac, her husband to be, we can be fairly sure, I think, that she'd ask Abraham's servant all sorts of questions about Isaac. I can only imagine that the servant was fulsome in praise of his master's son - all about his character and attributes and personality, and so on. I imagine Rebekah soaking it all up during that long camel ride. When the servant would talk of nearing home at last, I have the feeling that Rebekah, too, would almost be able to think of it in terms of coming home. Would she not have grown to love this man she'd never seen, but had heard so much about? The more she heard from the servant, the more she grew to love the master's son. It's the apostle Peter, writing in the New Testament, who says of our Lord Jesus *"whom not having seen we love"* (1 Peter 1:8).

I suggest that would fit the story of Rebekah travelling on to meet Isaac. As a Church, the Bride of Christ-to-be, believers on the Lord Jesus are travelling home to heaven and to the one whom not having seen we love; we love him already because of all that the Holy Spirit has revealed to our hearts about him. When in that sunset Isaac at last met his bride, surely his relationship with her would eclipse every other relationship in his life, even the particularly close one he'd had with his mother who'd recently died. Is it true of us, I wonder? Does our relationship with Christ eclipse every other relationship in our life?

# 11

# THE DEATHS OF SARAH & ABRAHAM

I'm sure you've been out for a meal with a friend who has insisted on paying. Being a Scotsman, that's the kind of friend I like to have! Our last look at Abraham finds him insisting on paying for something. Not a meal; but a grave or a burial plot. Abraham's wife, Sarah, has died, and although a burial plot for her is offered free of charge to Abraham by the people of the land (because of the esteem in which they held him), yet he refuses to accept this charity. Why? Could it have been pride? The missionary Jim Elliott thought a lot about this and one day recorded in his diary a very personal application he'd made from this incident. It made him realize, he said, that there's a cost to be paid in burying out of sight the dead things in our lives. This is how the Bible records the death of Sarah:

*"Sarah lived one hundred and twenty-seven years; these were the years of the life of Sarah. So Sarah died in Kirjath Arba (that is, Hebron) in the land of Canaan, and Abraham came to mourn for Sarah and to weep for her. Then Abraham stood up from before his dead, and spoke*

*to the sons of Heth, saying ... 'If it is your wish that I bury my dead out of my sight, hear me, and meet with Ephron the son of Zohar for me, that he may give me the cave of Machpelah which he has, which is at the end of his field. Let him give it to me at the full price, as property for a burial place among you.' Now Ephron dwelt among the sons of Heth; and Ephron the Hittite answered Abraham in the presence of the sons of Heth, all who entered at the gate of his city, saying, "No, my lord, hear me: I give you the field and the cave that is in it; I give it to you in the presence of the sons of my people. I give it to you. Bury your dead!"*

*Then Abraham bowed himself down before the people of the land; and he spoke to Ephron in the hearing of the people of the land, saying, 'If you will give it, please hear me. I will give you money for the field; take it from me and I will bury my dead there.' So the field of Ephron which was in Machpelah, which was before Mamre, the field and the cave which was in it, and all the trees that were in the field, which were within all the surrounding borders, were deeded to Abraham as a possession in the presence of the sons of Heth, before all who went in at the gate of his city. And after this, Abraham buried Sarah his wife in the cave of the field of Machpelah, before Mamre (that is, Hebron) in the land of Canaan. So the field and the cave that is in it were deeded to Abraham by the sons of Heth as property for a burial place'"* (Genesis 23:1-20).

Machpelah, the name of the place where Abraham buried Sarah, is an interesting word. It seems to have the meaning of 'double'.

The same word crops up later in the Bible in the description of the high priest's breasplate which was said to be 'doubled' (Exodus 39:9). So the cave of Machpelah where Abraham buried Sarah perhaps suggests to us a double cave. Some have pictured it as being like a cave with two entrances, or having both an entrance and an exit. Be that as it may, the last idea connects with the fact of resurrection - for the Bible says that the dead will be raised. Hebrews chapter 11 tells us of people like Sarah that "these all died in faith.".Surely that has to imply some sort of statement of their belief in resurrection, however hazy was their perception of something better beyond.

I don't know if you've heard the story told of the little boy who built a sailing boat and one day it was blown out to sea and lost. Sometime later, the story goes, he saw his boat priced for sale in a local shop window. There was nothing else to do, but save up his pocket money and buy it back. Then he could exclaim that it was 'twice his': for he had made it and then bought it back. The point often made is that God made us and, through his Son, also died to buy us back to himself. Have you discovered that you're twice God's? I do hope you have acknowledged that he made you and died for you in love.

Abraham could say about the land of the burial plot that it was now twice his.  It was his by promise and now by purchase. In fact, it seems this was the first, and very possibly the only, piece of the Promised Land that Abraham actually possessed for himself. It's as though all this is testimony to the fact that where he lived never mattered; but it did matter where Sarah died and was laid to rest. The Bible uses the expression at one point that the cave where Sarah was to be buried was 'at end of the field.' It actually says 'at the end of his field' in referring to it while it still belonged to Ephron, but it was the same field now in Abraham's possession where he buried Sarah. That seems to me to be a striking expression: 'at the end of his field or possession.'

Perhaps the only certainty in life is that at the end of all our possessions down here there lies a grave. Jesus Christ himself taught that life is not made up of the abundance of things we possess (Luke 12:15). Sometimes when the Bible gives us a list of names in a genealogy it includes repetitively (and rather obviously) 'and he died'; 'and he died'. That brings our mortality home to us. The prayer of Moses in Psalm 90 has the request: *"Teach us to number our days, that we may present to you a heart of wisdom"* (v.12).

It's important for us to be prepared to meet our God, as the Bible prophet urges (Amos 4:12), for the dead will be raised. That's what we've considered illustrated in the cave of Machpelah with its unusual name, meaning 'double' – and making us think of a way in and a way out. The story of Abraham ends with the Bible record of his own death:

> *"This is the sum of the years of Abraham's life which he lived: one hundred and seventy-five years. Then Abraham breathed his last and died in a good old age, an old man and full of years, and was gathered to his people. And his sons Isaac and Ishmael buried him in the cave of Machpelah, which is before Mamre, in the field of Ephron the son of Zohar the Hittite, the field which Abraham purchased from the sons of Heth. There Abraham was buried, and Sarah his wife"* (Genesis 25:7-10).

We have just read that Abraham "was gathered to his people". Sometimes in the Old Testament (e.g. Genesis 49:29-31) we read of another term "buried with his fathers". Perhaps the main thought in this latter one is the disposal of the body. But in the idea of being gathered to one's people, there is perhaps an indication pointing to the destiny of the soul. The complete record here is that Abraham 'breathed his last', was 'gathered to his people', and was 'buried.' It's as though this language reflects our threefold nature as spirit, soul and body. As to his spirit, Abraham breathed his last; as to his soul, he was gathered to his people; and, as to his body, he was buried. At death, our spirit returns to God who gave it (Ecclesiastes 12:7); our body returns to the earth and dust (Genesis 3:19); and our soul - if we know Jesus Christ as our personal Saviour - goes to be "with Christ" (Philippians 1:23).

So there we leave the story of Abraham. In so doing, we pick up once more on our concluding remarks, urging all to make sure of their soul's destiny by turning to God now, and believing in his Son, Jesus, for forgiveness.

# About the Publisher

Hayes Press (www.hayespress.org) is a registered charity in the United Kingdom, whose primary mission is to disseminate the Word of God, mainly through literature. It is one of the largest distributors of gospel tracts and leaflets in the United Kingdom, with over 100 titles and many thousands dispatched annually. In addition to paperbacks and eBooks, Hayes Press also publishes Golden Bells, a popular daily Bible reading calendar.

If you would like to contact Hayes Press, there are a number of ways you can do so:

By mail:  c/o The Barn, Flaxlands, Royal Wootton Bassett, Wiltshire, UK SN4 8DY

By phone: 01793 850598

By eMail: info@hayespress.org

via Facebook: www.facebook.com/hayespress.org

# About the Author

Born and educated in Scotland, Brian worked as a government scientist until God called him into full-time Christian ministry on behalf of the Churches of God (www.churchesofgod.info). His voice has been heard on Search For Truth radio broadcasts for over 30 years (visit www.searchfortruth.podbean.com) during which time he has been an itinerant Bible teacher throughout the UK. His evangelical and missionary work outside the UK is primarily in Belgium, The Philippines and South East Central Africa. He is married to Rosemary, with a son and daughter.

# Also by Brian Johnston

**No Room for Doubt**

In this innovative concise commentary on a key part of John's gospel, Brian imagines the Upper Room of John 13-17 as: The War-room, The Wash-room, The Dining-room, The Waiting-room, The Guest-room, The Plant-room, The Function-room and The Prayer-room.

**Can You Profess Christ and Still Be Lost?**

The eternal security of our salvation is a hotly debated topic amongst Christians today, Bible teacher and broadcaster Brian Johnston examines what the Bible has to say about whether it is possible to 'fall away' and how God wants us to be sure that we are saved.

- Law and Grace: Two Different Freedoms
- Is It Possible To Be a Carnal Christian?
- Is It a Case of 'No Holiness No Heaven'?
- Are Good Works Required for Salvation?
- Is It Possible to Fall Away?
- It's Not About How To Be Saved
- Is It Possible to Believe the Gospel in Vain?
- Once Saved, Always Saved
- The Different Tenses of Our Salvation

**Guardians of the Gate**

We join the writer of Chronicles as he records when God opened the way for his people to return from an enforced exile and to resume their previous temple service for Him in Jerusalem.    Brian explores the valuable lessons that we can learn from some of the background characters of Chronicles – including the zeal and the faithfulness of the temple gate-keepers who seem to have played a multi-faceted role, being the guards of the temple entrances, the supervising stewards of the people's contributions, the temple's night-watchmen, those responsible for admitting into its precincts only those who had a right to be there, the keepers of an inventory of the temple equipment, and the supervisors of the worship ingredients.